THE
NBA
A HISTORY OF HOOPS

Published by Creative Education
P.O. Box 227, Mankato, Minnesota 56002
Creative Education is an imprint of The Creative Company
www.thecreativecompany.us

Design and production by Christine Vanderbeek
Art direction by Rita Marshall

Printed by Corporate Graphics in the United States of America

Photographs by Corbis (Steve Lipofsky), Dreamstime (Munktcu), Getty
Images (Bill Baptist/NBAE, Andrew D. Bernstein/NBAE, Walter Bibikow,
Kevork Djansezian, Stephen Dunn, Jesse D. Garrabrant/NBAE, Otto
Greule Jr./Allsport, Glenn James/NBAE, Fernando Medina/NBAE, Layne
Murdoch/NBAE, Doug Pensinger, Mike Powell, Dick Raphael/NBAE,
SM/AIUEO), iStockphoto (Brandon Laufenberg)

Library of Congress Cataloging-in-Publication Data
Omoth, Tyler.
The story of the Dallas Mavericks / by Tyler Omoth.
p. cm. — (The NBA: a history of hoops)
Includes index.
Summary: The history of the Dallas Mavericks professional basketball
team from its start in 1980 to today, spotlighting the franchise's
greatest players and reliving its most dramatic moments.
ISBN 978-1-58341-941-0
1. Dallas Mavericks (Basketball team)—History—Juvenile literature. I. Title.
GV885.52.D34O46 2010   796.323'64097642812—dc22   2009034821

CPSIA: 120109 PO1093

First Edition
2 4 6 8 9 7 5 3 1

Page 3: Forwards Brandon Bass and Josh Howard
Pages 4–5: Forward Tim Thomas

THE STORY OF THE

DALLAS
MAVERICKS

TYLER OMOTH

CREATIVE C EDUCATION

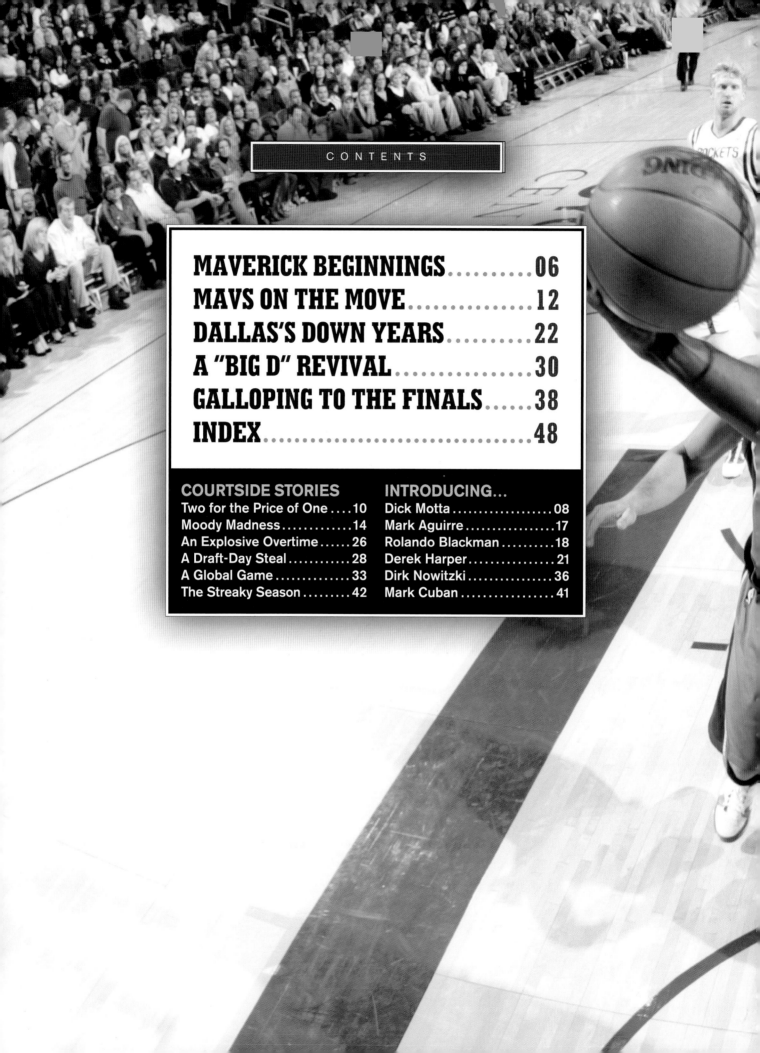

CONTENTS

CHAPTER ONE

MAVERICK BEGINNINGS

The city of Dallas, Texas, was born out of a spirit of adventure. When John Neely Bryan, a lawyer from Tennessee, discovered a spot that he believed had the perfect makings of a trading post in 1839, he claimed enough land to create a town. This maverick of his time was right. Dallas grew to become a vital inland port in the United States and a center for the oil and cotton industries. Today, the Dallas–Fort Worth–Arlington area comprises the fourth-largest metropolitan area in the U.S.

As the population grew in Dallas, so did the city's passion for sports. In 1960, the National Football League's Dallas Cowboys were created and quickly won the hearts of sports fans in "Big D" and throughout Texas. Later, the Texas Rangers Major League Baseball franchise moved into Arlington. In the late 1970s, talk began of a third major pro sport when businessmen Donald J. Carter and Norm Sonju recognized Dallas's sports fanaticism and pushed to bring big-time basketball to the city. After an ownership group headed by Carter paid a $12-million entry fee, the Dallas Mavericks were born in 1980 as part of the National Basketball Association (NBA).

Although sports fan in Dallas—and throughout Texas—are famously fond of football, Big D was quick to embrace the expansion Mavericks.

DICK MOTTA CLAIMED TO HAVE NEVER EVEN SEEN AN NBA GAME BEFORE SIGNING HIS FIRST NBA COACHING CONTRACT IN 1968. Regardless, he was the 1971 NBA Coach of the Year with the Chicago Bulls and won a championship in 1978 with the Washington Bullets. So when the fledgling Dallas Mavericks looked for their very first head coach, they tabbed him for the job. Although his players towered over him, the fiery Motta was a coach who demanded respect. In his interactions with the media, however, a more playful side of his personality often came out. "About three days into the training camp," he said of his first days with the expansion Mavericks franchise, "I was hoping that I could take some type of time tablet and play Rip Van Winkle, and have someone wake me up in three or four years!" By his fourth season as the Mavericks' coach, Motta had transformed Dallas into a playoff contender. The NBA's ninth-winningest coach of all time (as of 2010), Motta led the Mavs to the playoffs four times and oversaw the drafting of some of Dallas's most beloved stars.

INTRODUCING...

DICK MOTTA

COACH
MAVERICKS SEASONS
1980–87, 1994–96

The Mavericks were optimistic as they headed into their first season. Their head coach was Dick Motta, who just three years earlier had led the Washington Bullets to the NBA championship. Motta had a reputation as a demanding leader with a knack for wringing maximum effort out of his players. Dallas began building its original lineup by way of an expansion draft that let it select unprotected players from existing NBA rosters. The Mavericks used the opportunity to pick up such players as guard Austin Carr, forward Bingo Smith, and center Richard Washington.

In June 1980, the "Mavs" made forward Kiki Vandeweghe, out of the University of California, Los Angeles (UCLA), their very first collegiate acquisition via the NBA Draft, but Vandeweghe—anticipating some losing years in Dallas—refused to play for the expansion team. In December, Dallas would trade its rights to Vandeweghe and its 1986 first-round draft pick to the Denver Nuggets

EACH YEAR, EVERY TEAM IN THE NBA PUTS A LOT OF THOUGHT AND RESEARCH INTO ITS FIRST-ROUND PICK IN THE NBA DRAFT. The higher the pick, the more important it is. In 1980, the Dallas Mavericks were granted the 11th overall draft selection, which in theory meant they could get the 11th-best player available from the college ranks and make him the cornerstone of their new franchise. The Mavs chose high-scoring forward Kiki Vandeweghe from UCLA. Vandeweghe, however, had no intentions of signing with a fledgling franchise and immediately demanded to be traded. It was a tough blow to take, but the Mavericks set out to make the best of the situation. In December 1980, they traded the rights to Vandeweghe (plus their 1986 first-round draft choice) to the Nuggets for two future first-round draft picks. With those picks, the Mavs selected guard Rolando Blackman in 1981 and center Sam Perkins in 1984. Perkins became a solid performer at forward for six years in Dallas, and as of 2010, Blackman was the second-most prolific scorer in Mavericks history.

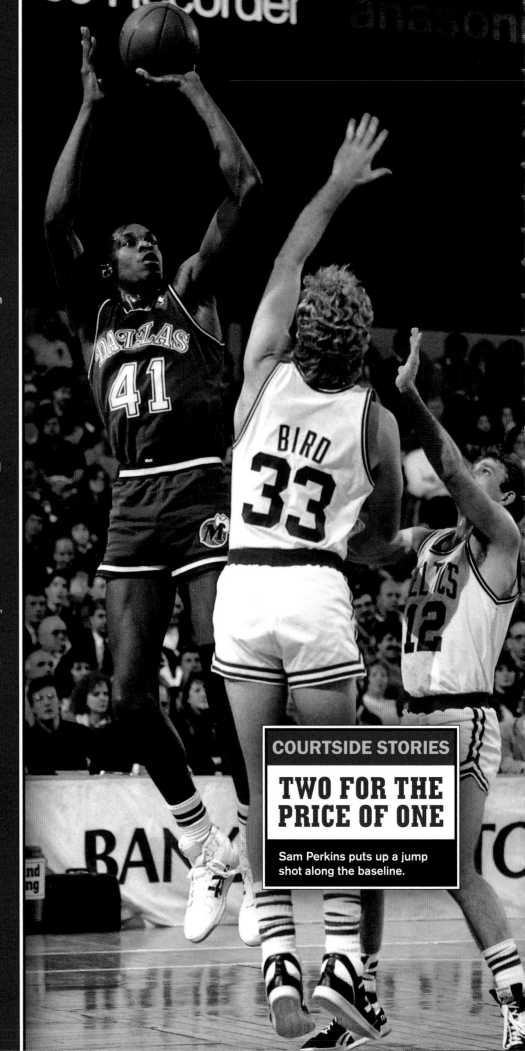

COURTSIDE STORIES

TWO FOR THE PRICE OF ONE

Sam Perkins puts up a jump shot along the baseline.

for two future first-round selections. As the Mavericks' first season unfolded, one of the few players who showed much in the way of talent was point guard Brad Davis, and even with Motta's coaching mojo, the Mavericks went just 15–67.

Dallas then selected three talented rookies in the 1981 NBA Draft: guard Rolando Blackman, swingman Mark Aguirre, and forward Jay Vincent. Blackman proved to be a fierce defender and a great outside shooter, while Aguirre and Vincent gave the team plenty of inside muscle. With the addition of these youngsters, the Mavericks showed quick and dramatic improvement, leaping to 28–54 in 1981–82 and 38–44 the following season. Things were beginning to look up in Big D.

In 1983, the Mavericks continued to enjoy tremendous success in the NBA Draft, adding guard Derek Harper. Harper had incredibly quick hands, which made him one of the league's best defenders. After spending his first few NBA seasons backing up Davis, he would become a permanent part of Dallas's starting lineup. "Derek is always ready to play at the end of a basketball game," said Blackman. "He's willing to be a hero. He's willing to be a goat—he doesn't care. You've got to get the basketball to guys like that."

CHAPTER TWO

MAVS ON THE MOVE

The Mavericks' improved talent level led to a rise in the Western Conference's Midwest Division standings. Dallas ended the 1983–84 season with the first winning record (43–39) in franchise history. That finish was good enough for second place in the division and earned the Mavericks their first playoff berth. Dallas beat the Seattle SuperSonics three games to two (winning Game 5 in overtime) in round one of postseason play. The Mavs' second-round opponent, however, was the scorching-hot Los Angeles Lakers, who defeated Dallas on their way to the NBA Finals.

The next year, the Mavericks drafted long-armed center Sam Perkins, who soon proved to be a force in the middle with his solid rebounding effort and knack for swatting away opposing shots. The team made the playoffs again with a 44–38 record but lost to the Portland Trail Blazers in the first round.

Brad Davis spent 12 seasons in a Mavericks uniform; in 1992, the franchise honored his loyalty and long service by retiring his jersey number.

COMEDIAN RODNEY DANGERFIELD WAS FAMOUS FOR THE LINE, "I GET NO RESPECT." Early Mavericks teams shared his plight: they just couldn't get any respect, even at home. When the Mavs made the playoffs in 1984, they had to play the deciding Game 5 of their first-round series against the Seattle SuperSonics at Moody Coliseum on the Southern Methodist University (SMU) campus, because their usual home, the much larger Reunion Arena, was booked for a tennis tournament. Mavs guard Rolando Blackman scored late in Game 5 to send it into overtime. With Dallas leading in the final seconds of overtime, Seattle forward Tom Chambers intercepted an inbound pass and heaved a desperate, 50-foot shot that missed, triggering a wild celebration among the Mavericks and their fans. However, the clock still showed 0.01. So, after officials consulted during a 14-minute delay, the referees pulled both teams out of their locker rooms to finish the game. The Mavericks defended Seattle's inbound pass to finally win the game and their first playoff series, giving rise to championship aspirations in Dallas. "It showed how far we had come as a franchise," said Blackman.

COURTSIDE STORIES

MOODY MADNESS

Rolando Blackman directs the offense from the point guard spot.

arly in the 1985–86 season, the Mavs traded for center James Donaldson. At a massive 7-foot-2, Donaldson gave Dallas intimidating size and strength in the low post. With his addition, the Mavs again went 44–38, then whipped the Utah Jazz in the first round of the playoffs before falling to the mighty Lakers in round two.

By 1986, Mavericks fans had grown accustomed to watching their team win during the regular season but get bounced from the playoffs. When the Mavs drafted towering forward Roy Tarpley, though, hopes rose. And when the Mavs' loaded lineup went 55–27 in 1986–87 and won the Midwest Division, an NBA championship seemed within reach. The excitement in Dallas came to an early and bitter halt, though, as the Mavs lost to the SuperSonics, three games to one, in a first-round playoff upset.

After that painful defeat, Motta stepped down as head coach. Dallas then hired coach John MacLeod to lead the Mavs to the next level. MacLeod did that more quickly than anyone expected, partly by

making Tarpley the team's sixth man. By coming off the

bench late in the game, Tarpley often dominated his tired

opponents. "With Roy on the floor, we talk NBA champi-

onship," said Blackman. "He brings us that little piece of

magic … you see in a player who is superior to everyone

he plays against."

In the 1988 playoffs, Tarpley and the Mavs earned victo-

ries over the Houston Rockets and Denver Nuggets.

The only team standing between them and the NBA

Finals was their old nemesis, the Lakers. In a titanic battle,

the two teams split the first six games of the Western

Conference finals, but the more experienced Lakers won

Game 7 by a 117–102 score. Los Angeles went on to win

the NBA championship, while the Mavs again went home

empty-handed.

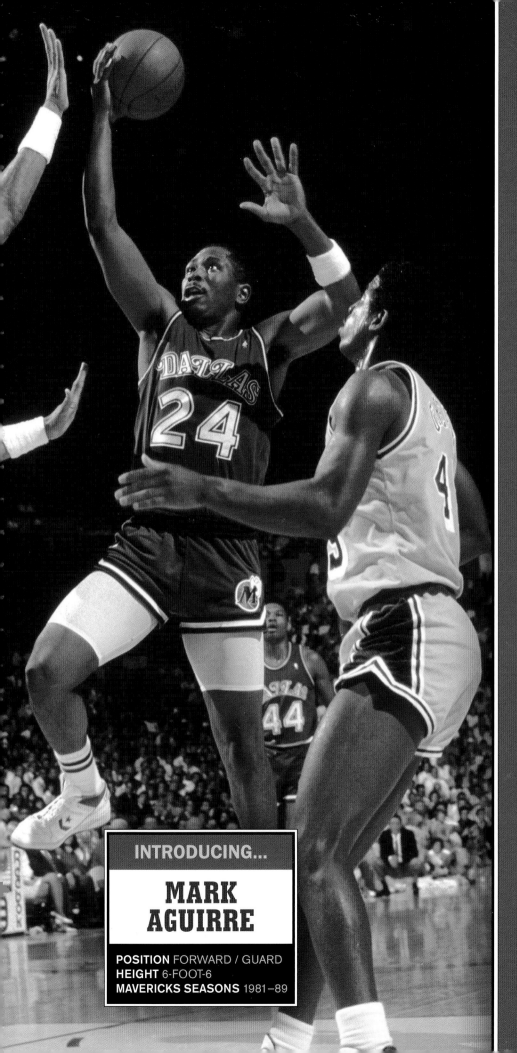

SOMETIMES IT'S HELPFUL FOR A BASKETBALL TEAM TO HAVE A PLAYER WITH A NASTY SIDE. Before the Mavericks made Mark Aguirre from DePaul University the number-one overall pick in the 1981 NBA Draft, they'd seen his skills on the court, and they'd heard about his sometimes surly attitude. Aguirre was never a player who went out of his way to be the most-liked player in the NBA, but what he did do was score. At 6-foot-6 and 235 pounds, he was considerably stockier than the league's prototypical player. Over the course of his career, he averaged 20 points per game, and as of 2010, he held the Mavericks' single-season scoring record with 2,330 points (in 1983–84). On several occasions, the prickly star butted heads with coach Dick Motta, but in the end, Aguirre's scoring ability kept the Mavericks and their fans happy. "He was a passer, he was a power player inside, and he played against bigger people," said Dallas coach John MacLeod. "And then he had the ability to drive the ball to the basket. He was a complete player."

INTRODUCING...

ROLANDO BLACKMAN

POSITION GUARD
HEIGHT 6-FOOT-6
MAVERICKS SEASONS 1981–92

WHEN THE MAVERICKS SELECTED ROLANDO BLACKMAN NINTH OVERALL IN THE 1981 NBA DRAFT, DALLAS WAS A YOUNG TEAM THAT BADLY NEEDED A HERO. It found one in the slick-shooting guard from Kansas State University. High-strung and always intense, Blackman was never lacking in confidence. As an unproven rookie, he boldly predicted that he'd be a star and that he couldn't be guarded. He became a great scorer, but his intensity made him a tenacious defensive player as well. Blackman helped to form the foundation of a Mavericks team that was consistently a force to be reckoned with in the mid-1980s. From 1984 to 1990, the Mavericks missed the playoffs only once, while Blackman earned All-Star status four times. Blackman retired as the Mavericks' all-time leading scorer after 11 seasons with the team and 2 more with the New York Knicks. Lakers Hall-of-Famer Magic Johnson recalled playing against Blackman, calling him "one of the greatest shooters of all time and one of the most difficult players to guard." It turned out that Blackman's prediction was as accurate as his shot.

Still, Dallas fans were as enthusiastic as ever heading into the 1988–89 season. Their team had made the playoffs five straight years, inching closer to the NBA Finals every time. But everything then fell apart. First, Tarpley was suspended for drug abuse. Then Aguirre demanded to be traded and was dealt to the Detroit Pistons for a player—forward Adrian Dantley—who at first refused to play for Dallas. To top it all off, Donaldson suffered a serious knee injury.

In just a few weeks, the team chemistry that Dallas had worked so long to build was almost completely destroyed. Even though Dantley eventually suited up for Dallas, and Tarpley returned from his suspension, the damage was done. The Mavericks missed the 1989 playoffs, made a brief comeback the next season with a 47–35 record, and then suffered a first-round playoff exit. Little did Dallas fans know that their team was about to fall into a long, agonizing slump and that the Mavericks wouldn't make the playoffs again for more than a decade.

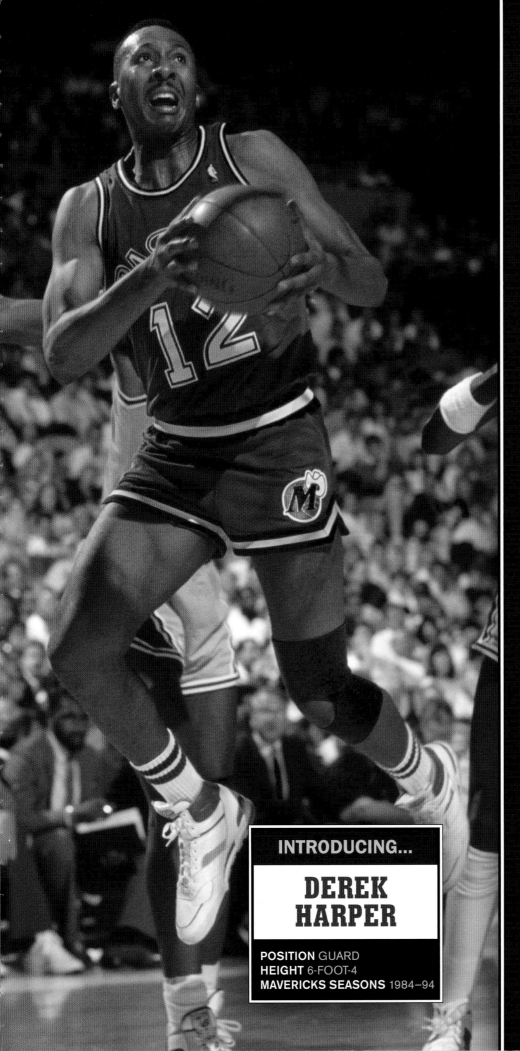

INTRODUCING...

DEREK HARPER

POSITION GUARD
HEIGHT 6-FOOT-4
MAVERICKS SEASONS 1984–94

SOME PLAYERS HELP THEIR TEAM WITHOUT HAVING SUPERSTAR STATISTICS. They're sometimes called the "glue guys," because they're the players who hold a team together. For 10 seasons, Derek Harper was a glue guy for the Dallas Mavericks. On a team that featured the volatile Mark Aguirre and the overly energetic Rolando Blackman, Harper provided steady scoring and steely defense. Whenever the Mavs would face a superstar guard, shutting him down would be Harper's assignment. In 1986, he became the first Dallas player ever named to the NBA's All-Defensive team. In typical glue-guy fashion, if something broke, Harper found a way to fix it. Late in Game 4 of the second round of the 1984 playoffs, he made an embarrassing mistake by dribbling out the clock, thinking that the Mavericks were leading the Lakers when, in fact, the game was tied. The Lakers went on to win. Two years later, in another round-two matchup against the Lakers, Harper made up for it by draining two three-pointers in the final minute of Game 3 to win the game and keep the Mavericks alive in the series.

CHAPTER THREE

DALLAS'S DOWN YEARS

Dallas lost Perkins via free agency in 1990, and a 1990–91 season riddled with injuries saw the Mavericks fall to 28–54. The following season started out with a shock for Mavericks players and fans, as Tarpley was banned from the NBA in October for his third violation of the league's substance abuse policy. The aging, oft-injured team then sank even lower, managing just 22 wins. After the season, Dallas began to part ways with its veterans and to build for the future with younger players. Blackman, a favorite among fans and within the Dallas locker room, was sent to the New York Knicks for a first-round draft pick.

Despite the best efforts of such players as rugged rebounder Terry Davis, Dallas became a basketball disaster in the early '90s, putting up the embarrassing records of 11–71 and 13–69 in 1992–93 and 1993–94. The team's youth and

Drug abuse and injuries reduced Roy Tarpley's potential to a story of what might have been, as he played in parts of only six NBA seasons.

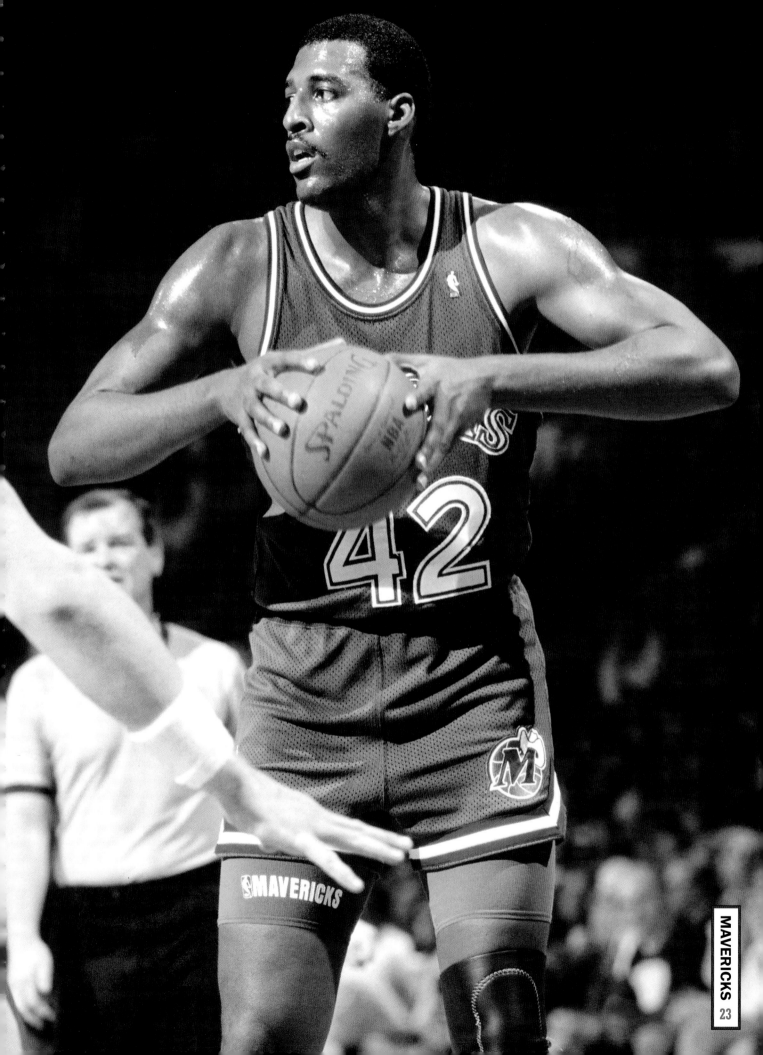

lack of leadership was evident in its play, and the Mavs simply couldn't compete in a league where experience and teamwork were every bit as important as athleticism. Only late-season victories each year kept the Mavericks from setting a new NBA record for the fewest wins in a season.

The only silver lining to the Mavs' horrible seasons of the early '90s was that, by finishing at the bottom of the standings, the team consistently "earned" high picks in the annual NBA Draft. Dallas used these picks to stockpile some of the nation's best college players. From 1992 to 1994, the Mavs drafted three outstanding young players: guard Jim Jackson, forward Jamal Mashburn, and point guard Jason Kidd.

In 1994–95, the Mavs at last showed signs of life by assembling a respectable 36–46 mark. Part of the credit went to such players as big forward Popeye Jones. The driving force behind this improvement, however, was the team's "Three J's"—Jim, Jamal, and Jason. Jackson and Mashburn combined to score more than 50 points a game, while Kidd dished out 7.7 assists per game and was named NBA Co-Rookie of the Year (along with Detroit Pistons forward Grant Hill).

Jackson and Mashburn were clearly talented, but Kidd was the brightest star of them all and the engine that drove the team. At 6-foot-4 and 210 pounds, Kidd could do it all: run the fast break, score, rebound, and shut down opposing guards on the defensive end of the court. Even Chicago Bulls star guard Michael Jordan called Kidd "the future" of the NBA. In 1995–96, Kidd backed up the hype by averaging 16.6 points and 9.7 assists—many of them in alley-oop, behind-the-back, or "no-look" fashion—per game.

Sadly, this great collection of talent would largely go to waste. Mashburn suffered a serious knee injury in 1995, and personality clashes among players began to tear the team apart. In 1996, Dallas hired a new coach, Jim Cleamons, and installed a new half-court offense. Kidd, who preferred a faster-paced offense that allowed him to create plays in the open court, did not adapt well to the change. All of these problems

SOMETIMES NBA FANS GET MORE THAN THEY PAY FOR. When the Mavericks faced their intrastate rivals, the Houston Rockets, on April 11, 1995, Dallas was 34–41 and considered an underdog to the 44–32 Rockets. On this night, however, the two teams were evenly matched. The Mavericks pulled away and appeared headed for a comfortable victory before the Rockets rallied to score 18 points in the final 70 seconds of regulation to tie the game at 119–119. In the first overtime, it was the Mavericks' turn to erupt. They scored 11 points in the last 55 seconds, including a trio of 3-point shots from guard Jason Kidd, to send the game to double overtime. The Mavericks rode that momentum into the second overtime and defeated the Rockets by a final score of 156–147. The two teams combined for 46 points in the first overtime period, which remained an NBA record as of 2010. "I've never played in a game like this," said a tired Kidd. "I hope it will be the last."

COURTSIDE STORIES

AN EXPLOSIVE OVERTIME

Jamal Mashburn elevates for a jumper against the Rockets.

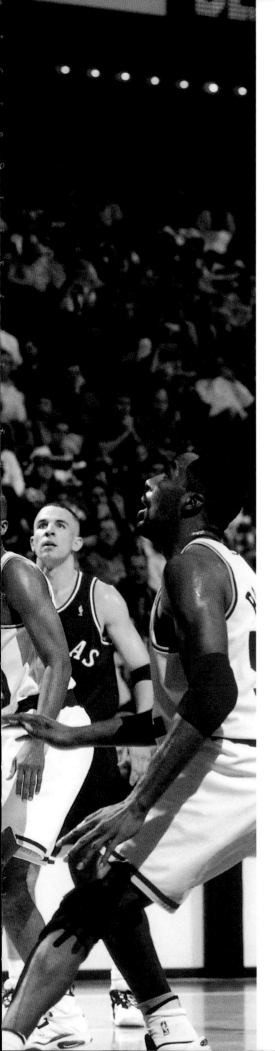

triggered a major housecleaning in Dallas. In a rapid series of stunning moves, the Mavericks traded away Kidd, Mashburn, and Jackson.

Among the new faces in town after all the personnel maneuvers were one of the NBA's leading shot blockers, 7-foot-6 center Shawn Bradley, speedy point guard Robert Pack, and high-scoring swingman Michael Finley. Also on the roster was an undrafted free agent, guard Erick Strickland, who contributed 10.6 points per game in 1996–97, eighth-best among all NBA rookies.

After Dallas started 4–12 during the 1997–98 season, general manager Don Nelson replaced Cleamons as Dallas's head coach. In an entertaining yet frustrating season, the Mavericks pulled off a number of upsets but could muster only 20 wins en route to losing 62 games. During the off-season, Nelson and the Mavs began to pursue players around whom they could construct a winning lineup. In a trade with the Phoenix Suns, Dallas found one such player, securing a proven on-court leader by acquiring guard Steve Nash. "He's going to be our point guard," said Nelson. "He'll be terrific in our system."

A DRAFT-DAY STEAL

Guard Steve Nash slips past a
defender to make an assist.

WHERE DOES A TEAM LOOK WHEN IT WANTS TO MAKE A STEAL OF A TRADE? Why not to the team that traded legendary center Kareem Abdul-Jabbar away in 1975? Or the team that drafted highflying forward Julius "Dr. J" Erving, only to watch him slip through its fingers in 1972? The Milwaukee Bucks were on the unfortunate end of both of those deals, and in 1998,

they were willing to swap again. Dallas orchestrated a three-team trade that gave Milwaukee the rights to the sixth pick in that year's NBA Draft, which the Bucks used to grab beefy University of Michigan forward Robert "Tractor" Traylor. The Mavericks ended up with the rights to forwards Dirk Nowitzki and Pat Garrity. Dallas immediately turned around and traded Garrity to

the Phoenix Suns for point guard Steve Nash. Garrity became a solid bench player for a decade, and Traylor assembled a mediocre seven-year NBA career. Nash, meanwhile, tallied a whopping 2,919 career assists in a Dallas uniform, and Nowitzki went on to win the 2007 NBA MVP award, making the blockbuster deal a major steal for the Mavericks.

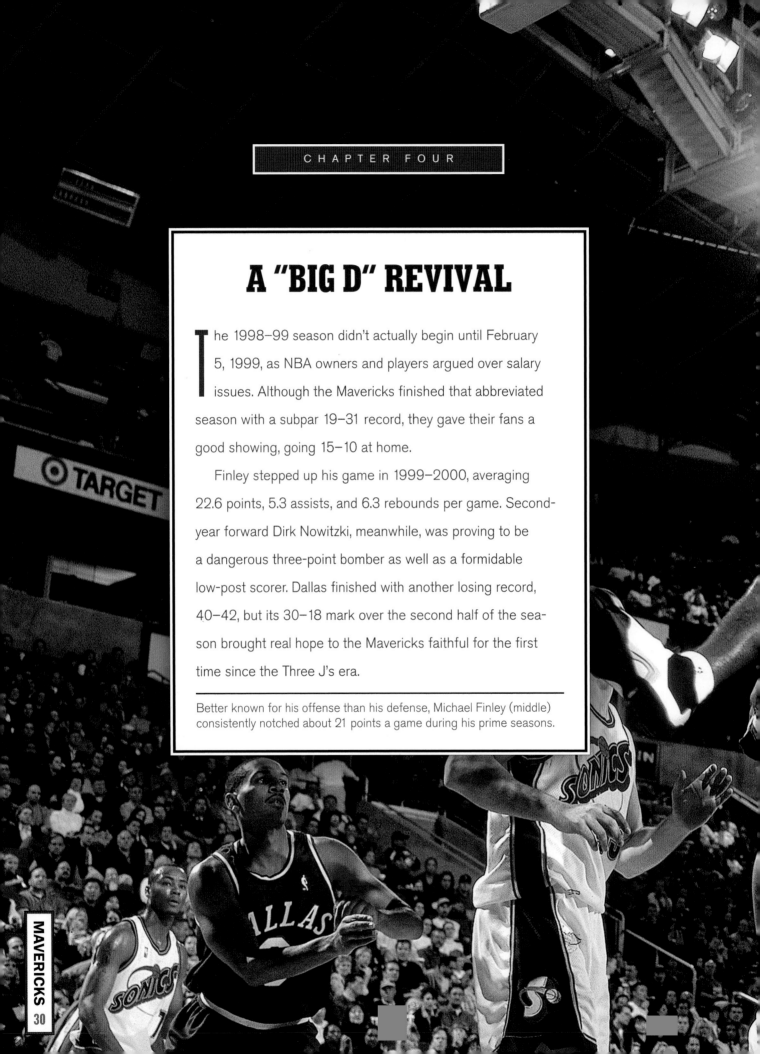

CHAPTER FOUR

A "BIG D" REVIVAL

The 1998–99 season didn't actually begin until February 5, 1999, as NBA owners and players argued over salary issues. Although the Mavericks finished that abbreviated season with a subpar 19–31 record, they gave their fans a good showing, going 15–10 at home.

Finley stepped up his game in 1999–2000, averaging 22.6 points, 5.3 assists, and 6.3 rebounds per game. Second-year forward Dirk Nowitzki, meanwhile, was proving to be a dangerous three-point bomber as well as a formidable low-post scorer. Dallas finished with another losing record, 40–42, but its 30–18 mark over the second half of the season brought real hope to the Mavericks faithful for the first time since the Three J's era.

Better known for his offense than his defense, Michael Finley (middle) consistently notched about 21 points a game during his prime seasons.

Playing under new team owner Mark Cuban, the Mavs finally broke their playoff drought. Dallas, the worst team in basketball just a handful of seasons before, suddenly became an NBA powerhouse. After trading for veteran forward Juwon Howard, Dallas cruised to a 53–29 mark and made the 2001 playoffs—its first postseason berth since 1990. The starting five of Nash, Finley, Nowitzki, Howard, and Bradley led the Mavericks past the Utah Jazz in the first round but were unable to get past the San Antonio Spurs in round two. The Mavericks, though, were only starting to run.

The Mavs tipped off 2001–02 in a new home, having left Reunion Arena for the new, state-of-the-art American Airlines Center, and Dallas fans had reason to believe their Mavericks might decorate their new digs with a championship banner. For the second consecutive year, the Mavs pulled the trigger on a midseason trade, sending Howard

THANKS IN PART TO THE ENORMOUS FOLLOWING OF THE U.S. OLYMPIC "DREAM TEAMS" DURING THE 1992 AND 1996 SUMMER OLYMPICS, BASKETBALL'S GLOBAL POPULARITY WAS SOARING BY THE END OF THE 1990S. Eight international players were chosen in the 2000 NBA Draft, and seven were taken the next year. Perhaps no team embraced the multinational blending of the NBA like the Dallas Mavericks. When the Mavs took the court for the 2001–02 season, they featured one of the most nationally diverse rosters in league history. Their slick-passing point guard, Steve Nash, hailed from Canada (though he was actually born in South Africa). The team's star forward, Dirk Nowitzki, was from Germany and manned the frontcourt with Chinese center Wang Zhizhi. Mexican forward Eduardo Najera and French guard Tariq Abdul-Wahad, meanwhile, rounded out what was a very talented team. "Having players that are national heroes adds quite a bit to the team," Mavericks owner Mark Cuban said of his squad. "Having a whole country counting on you to represent them and win is a whole lot more pressure than an NBA playoff game."

and two other players to the Nuggets for forward Raef LaFrentz and guards Nick Van Exel and Avery Johnson. With these players supporting the three-pronged attack of Nash, Nowitzki, and Finley, the Mavericks surged to 57 wins. They swept the Minnesota Timberwolves in the first round but fell short of the NBA Finals again as the Sacramento Kings then defeated them four games to one.

The Mavs continued their upward climb. In 2002–03, Dallas became the first team in the NBA to clinch a playoff spot, securing its bid by mid-March and finishing with a 60–22 record—tied for the best in the NBA with the Spurs. After defeating the Trail Blazers in the first round of the playoffs, the Mavericks knocked out the Kings in seven games to advance to the Western Conference finals for the first time since 1988. Unfortunately, star forward Tim Duncan and the Spurs proved to be too much for the Mavericks, and Dallas fell four games to two. "It was a matter of them turning their gear up a level, and we couldn't get any higher," explained Dallas coach Don Nelson. "That was the end of it."

More trades then followed as Van Exel and LaFrentz left, and forwards Antoine Walker and Antawn Jamison arrived. Opposing defenses

could no longer worry about just three Mavs stars, as Nash, Nowitzki, Finley, Jamison, and Walker each scored more than 14 points per game during the season. For the fourth year in a row, Dallas won more than 50 games, but the Mavs continued to stumble in the postseason as the Kings sent them home in the first round.

True to form, the Mavericks did not sit idly by as they prepared for the next season. Jamison and Walker were traded, and Nash left town as a free agent. Guard Jason Terry and forward Jerry Stackhouse were brought in via trades, and Dallas obtained fast point guard Devin Harris via the NBA Draft. With improved play from second-year forward Josh Howard, the Mavericks put together a 58–24 record to earn a fifth consecutive playoff appearance. Unfortunately, after defeating the Rockets in seven games in the first round, the Mavericks were bested by Nash and his new team, the Suns, in the second round.

POSITION FORWARD
HEIGHT 7 FEET
MAVERICKS SEASONS 1998–PRESENT

DIRK NOWITZKI